The Power of Peace

Protection & Direction

VIKKI BURKE

Dennis Burke Publications

The Power of Peace—Protection and Direction
ISBN 1-890026-09-3
© 1999 by Dennis Burke Publications
PO Box 150043
Arlington, TX 76015

Unless otherwise indicated, all Scripture
quotations are taken from the *New American
Standard Bible*.

Your Guard and Umpire

Fellowship with man is God's greatest desire. Nothing is more important to Him or more vital to our well-being in this life.

But people struggle with this. Some are not comfortable talking to God. Others have trouble believing they could ever hear His voice. It is because they have either lost or never possessed the one gift that would protect their ability to fellowship with God. They aren't taking advantage of this gift designed to protect what the Bible calls the heart, or spirit, of man.

This gift is the one thing that can filter out the clamor, confusion and conflicting demands of the world in which they live. Desire for it knows no social barrier. If it could be purchased, every wealthy person on earth would obtain it.

The gift is God's gift of peace. Obtaining it and letting it do what God created it to do is the most important thing anyone can ever do for the sake of his or her heart.

Like a soldier guards a city to keep out enemies and intruders,

God has given you the gift of a powerful protector to guard your heart. But this gift can only work if you let it.

God's peace, as the Bible describes it, is a life-changing force given two vital assignments related to your heart. First it is assigned to guard your heart:

> God's peace...which transcends all understanding shall garrison and mount guard over your hearts and minds in Christ Jesus (Philippians 4:6-7, *The Amplified Bible*).

A second assignment is to act as umpire—helping you to

make the right decision in challenging situations. The Apostle Paul says,

> Let the peace (soul harmony which comes) from Christ rule (act as an umpire continually) in your hearts [deciding and settling with finality all questions that arise in your minds] (Colossians 3:15, *The Amplified Bible*).

Make Peace with God

So how do you get, and keep, this gift of peace from God?

The first thing you must do to

6

find peace is to *make* peace with your Creator. God created mankind for the purpose of fellowship. But Adam's sin created a barrier between mankind and God. Jesus came to earth to bear the sin of man, breaking the barrier that separated them.

By receiving Jesus as your Lord, you make peace with God. Romans 10:9-10 says,

> If you confess with your mouth Jesus as Lord, and believe in your heart that God raised Him from the dead, you shall be saved; for with the heart man believes, resulting in righteousness, and with

the mouth he confesses, resulting in salvation.

Simply pray this from your heart, and God will accept you as His child.

Ephesians 2:8 says,

You have this new relationship with God simply by accepting it. It is his gift to you through his unconditional love. It is not something you could ever earn by any effort of your own, so you can't brag about having it, or about doing anything (*Ben Campbell Johnson Paraphrase*).

When you ask Jesus to be your Lord and mean it from your heart, then you have entered the family of God. Verse 19 says,

> You are no longer outsiders or aliens, but on the inside with the insiders; you have a place in the family of God.

Jesus said,

> Peace I leave with you; My peace I give to you; not as the world gives, do I give to you. Let not your heart be troubled, nor let it be fearful (John 14:27).

The world doesn't have ac-

9

cess to this peace; it is only available to those who make Jesus their Lord and become members of the family of God. It is made available as a force that comes alive only within the reborn human spirit.

A Supernatural Force

When you become a Christian, God deposits into your heart forces the Bible calls the fruit of the spirit. Galatians 5:22-25 says,

> But the fruit of the Spirit is love, joy, *peace*, patience, kindness, goodness, faithfulness, gentleness, self-control; against such things there is no

law. Now those who belong to Christ Jesus have crucified the flesh with its passions and desires. If we live by the Spirit, let us also walk by the Spirit.

Just like fruit originates from within a tree, so the force of peace is generated from within the recreated human spirit. Our task is to learn to yield to these forces instead of continuing to act the way we have in the past. Instead of living by the impulses of the flesh, we must learn to live by the spirit.

Drawing on the force of peace from within our spirit doesn't happen automatically.

Just like anything else in life it takes practice. It involves a choice.

When we sense the urge to give way to the flesh, we must choose instead to yield to peace—the fruit of the spirit.

Watch Out for Intruders

Of course, one great help in this process is to learn how to recognize and guard our hearts from intruders that would steal our peace. Proverbs 4:23 says,

> Keep your heart with all diligence, for out of it spring the issues of life *(New King James).*

What are some of those major intruders?

One is the emphasis on outward appearances. Instead of giving attention to the spirit, people give in to the great emphasis and value the world places on outward appearance. Most people give more attention to what they look like or appear to be than they do to the well-being of the inward life.

This focus on outward appearance has created deep-seated feelings of inadequacy for many. It creates a paralyzing inertia, stealing any motivation and joy they might have had. The inward issues of the heart are left unattended and peace is sacrificed. This indiscretion is very costly!

The answer is to see ourselves from God's perspective. When God sent Samuel to the house of Jesse to anoint one of his sons as king, He said,

> Do not look at his appearance or at the height of his stature, because I have rejected him; for God sees not as man sees, for man looks at the outward appearance, but the Lord looks at the heart (1 Samuel 16:7).

The book of Peter reveals

God's attitude toward outward appearance. It says,

> Let not yours be the [merely] external adorning with [elaborate] interweaving and knotting of the hair, the wearing of jewelry, or changes of clothes; but let it be the inward adorning and beauty of the hidden person of the heart, with the incorruptible and unfading charm of a gentle and peaceful spirit, which [is not anxious or wrought up, but] is very precious in the sight of God (I Peter 3:3-4, *The Amplified Bible*).

Peter was prompting them to look beyond the shallow issues to the more important, inward adorning. He said that a gentle, peaceful heart is very precious in the sight of God. If it's precious to God, then it should be precious to His children.

Avoid Overcrowding

People also lose their peace in another way—by measuring themselves by their performance. They haven't separated *who* they are from what they *do*.

I have noticed recently that when I ask someone the question, "How are you?" often their answer is, "Busy." That statement might sound innocent, but it can be a sign of a greater problem. If it hasn't already, it will cause distress and anxiety that result in a life that has become overwhelmed.

There are a variety of reasons for becoming too busy. Many simply live a lifestyle that requires an unreasonable amount of time. One person may be too busy because of the demands of a growing career added to the needs of his or her family—needs such as homework, sports and other activities.

Others become too busy because they are unable to say no when asked to do something.

Still others get their sense of worth from being needed, so they fill their lives with doing for others. Whatever the reason, when you're too busy, your mind becomes a prisoner to what you must do next—constantly thinking and planning. Satan will try to use an overly busy life to choke out the promise of God and keep you from producing spiritually (see Mark 4:18-19).

The most important thing in your life is not your performance naturally, but your fruitfulness spiritually. I'm not saying that God doesn't want you to be productive while you're on earth. But it does mean that He is more interested in your peace than your achievements. God knows that if your heart is right, eventually your performance will be too.

Reject Regret

Another reason people fail to live in peace is they will not let go of the failure from their past.

Regret debilitates and destroys. With regret comes self-condemnation, shame, grief, sorrow and torment. When you are in Christ, no matter what you have done in your past, when you repent it is removed as far as the east is from the west (see Psalm 103:12).

Based upon what Jesus did

on the cross, God is willing to remove your past. You should forget the past too. Romans 8:1 says,

> No condemnation now hangs over the head of those who are 'in' Christ Jesus. For the new principle of life in Christ Jesus lifts me out of the old vicious cycle of sin and death (*J.B. Phillips*).

Regret is accompanied by grief. But Isaiah 53:4-5 says,

> Surely our griefs He himself bore, and our sorrows He carried; yet we ourselves esteemed Him

stricken, smitten of God, and afflicted. But He was pierced through for our transgressions, He was crushed for our iniquities; the chastening for our well-being fell upon Him, and by His scourging we are healed.

Jesus not only bore your sin, but He bore your grief and sorrow as well. You could say He bore your regret; you should not bear it too.

God is not holding past failures against us. He's not asking us to decide if an issue is too big or too small to give to Him. Heart issues are important to Him.

He wants us to have peaceful hearts that can hear His voice and enjoy fellowship with Him.

The Heart Issue

As we read in Proverbs 4:23, God gives a strict charge to "keep (guard) your heart with all diligence." The word *keep* means "to hedge about, guard, protect and attend to."

Genesis 2:15 records the event when the Lord God put man in the Garden of Eden to cultivate it and keep it. Adam's job was to be watchful of anything that may threaten his garden. He was to post a guard to keep out all intruders.

That is just what we are supposed to do for our hearts. Our eyes and ears are the gateways to our hearts. Therefore, we must protect what goes in our eyes and ears because it has the potential of stealing our peace.

There is good cause for keeping your heart—your life depends on it! Verse 23 says it is from out of the heart that the issues of life spring. From a well-kept heart flows living issues like health, joy, peace and love.

Philippians 4:6-7 says,

Do not fret or have any anxiety about anything, but in every circumstance and in everything, by prayer and petition (definite requests), with thanksgiving, continue to make your wants known to God. And God's peace...which transcends all understanding shall garrison and mount guard over your hearts and minds in Christ Jesus *(The Amplified Bible).*

Like a soldier guards a city to keep out enemies and intruders, peace has a job to do. Peace can only do its job when you refuse to fret and be anxious about anything! Instead, Paul exhorts you to pray over *everything.*

The only way peace will mount guard over your heart is when you concede to God in every circumstance. Proverbs 3:5-6 says,

> Trust in the Lord with all your heart, and do not lean on your own understanding. In all your ways acknowledge Him, and He will make your paths straight.

Your trust cannot be in your understanding or ability to fix a situation; it must be in the Lord. God wants involvement in every area of your life.

Jesus said the foremost commandment is to love the Lord your God with all your heart, all your soul, all your mind and all your strength. That means give Him all you've got. When you do, the peace of God that transcends mental understanding will not only flood your being, but it will mount guard over your heart and mind.

When trouble comes knocking at your door, the peace that comes from God has the assignment and the power to stand guard to answer and take control of the situation. All it needs is your agreement. You must allow peace to do its job. You are the deciding factor.

Let Your Umpire Make the Calls

Not only will your decision allow peace to guard your heart, but it will also allow peace to act as an umpire over those situations that Satan would use to steal your peace. The Apostle Paul says,

> Let the peace (soul harmony which comes) from Christ rule (act as an umpire continually) in your hearts [deciding and settling with finality all questions that arise in your minds] (Colossians 3:15, *The Amplified Bible*).

Imagine a baseball game between two highly competitive teams that was being played without an umpire. You don't have to be an avid baseball fan to realize that game would quickly end up in chaos. Each team would insist the close plays be called to their advantage and would stretch the limits of the rules in their favor.

It is in the interest of both teams to have someone outside the situation who has been empowered to bring order and keep the game moving on toward its goal.

An umpire is one called on

when things do not agree to settle a controversy or question between parties—a person se-
lected to decide all disputed
points.

Letting peace be your umpire
means when the doctor gives
you an evil report that doesn't
agree with the Word of God, you
let the umpire settle the question.

When people hurt and op-
pose you, let the supernatural
peace that comes from God
alone make the calls in those
situations. In this earth, you will
always be responding to opposi-
tion, offense and confusion. But
a powerful gift from God can
make your responses easier.

At Peace with Others

The fact is that as long as you are on the earth, other people are going to hurt and disappoint you. But if you choose beforehand to let peace rule in those situations, those hurts and disappointments will not have opportunity to enter your heart. You keep them at arm's length.

It takes effort not to become hurt and offended at others. The only way we can do it is to yield to the fruit of the spirit. The importance of this is we cannot have quality fellowship with God when we are in constant conflict with others.

How do you let peace be an umpire in those times of disappointment? Choose to forgive and turn the resolving of those issues and the ordering of your emotions over to God. Jesus said,

> And whenever you stand praying, forgive, if you have anything against anyone; so that your Father also who is in heaven may forgive you your transgressions. But if you do not forgive, neither will your Father who is in heaven forgive your transgressions (Mark 11:25-26).

Forgiveness is not complete until we have aggressively pursued peace at all costs.

Hebrews 12:14 says,

Pursue peace with all men and the sanctification without which no one will see the Lord.

It may take several times saying and determining in your heart, "I will not be hurt or offended, I choose to forgive." But the effort is well worth it, and the alternative is costly.

To refuse to forgive is to choose to yield to the flesh. The person who takes this path is in essence rejecting God's help and taking the situation into his own hands. He is trusting in the ability of man.

Allowing ourselves to be hurt, disappointed, frustrated and offended by others greatly impairs our ability to see God working in our lives. Jeremiah 17:5-6 says,

> Thus says the Lord: Cursed [with great evil] is the strong man who trusts in and relies on frail man, making weak [human] flesh his arm, and whose mind and heart turn aside from the Lord. For he shall be like a shrub or a person naked and desti-

tute in the desert; and he shall not see any good come; but shall dwell in the parched places in the wilderness, in an uninhab- ited salt land (*The Ampli- fied Bible*).

The person who does not pur- sue peace with all men, but trusts and relies on weak human ability is unable to see when good comes into his or her life.

The Living Bible puts it this way: "The good times pass him by forever."

However, look at what hap- pens to the one who trusts in the Lord:

[Most] blessed is the man who believes in, trusts in and relies on the Lord, and whose hope and confidence the Lord is. For he shall be like a tree planted by the waters, that spreads out its roots by the river; and it shall not see and fear when heat comes; but his leaf shall be green. It shall not be anxious and full of care in the year of drought, nor shall it cease yielding fruit (Jer. 17:7-8, *The Amplified Bible*).

This person not only survives the heat and drought, but he also never ceases to yield fruit.

Many people blame God for the trouble in their lives. The truth is, in the pressure situations we face, it's the choices *we* make that determine the results we get. God doesn't have much to do with it.

Work Hard at Living in Peace

Romans 12:18 says, "If possible, so far as it depends on you, be at peace with all men." Other people can make it difficult to be at peace with them, and sometimes they will not be at peace with us. But as far as we are concerned, we are to be at peace with them.

About ten years ago, the wife of one of my relatives left him so devastated that he bought a gun and threatened to kill himself. However, he was arrested and put into the hospital. The hospital could only legally keep him forty-eight hours. When he was released, he bought another gun and made the same threats. Again he was arrested and hospitalized for forty-eight hours. When released, he repeated the same behavior a third time.

Because I lived in another state, my family called to keep me informed about what was happening during these three events. Dennis and I agreed in prayer over the situation according to Matthew 18:18-19:

> Believe me, whatever you forbid upon earth will be what is forbidden in Heaven, and whatever you permit on earth will be what is permitted in Heaven.
>
> And I tell you once more that if two of you on earth agree in asking for anything it will be granted to you by my Heavenly Father (*J. B. Phillips*).

Agreeing in prayer, we forbade the spirit of suicide to take his life. I had to draw on the force of peace in order to keep from flying out there so I could *do* something. But the truth was, my prayers *were* doing something. According to the scripture we just read, when we forbade him to take his life, all of heaven backed us up! What dynamic power is available to a believer!

During that time the Lord spoke something very unusual to me. He said, "Don't fly out there. Make him hungry for what you have." In the natural realm I didn't know how to do that. So I prayed in the spirit, knowing that 1 Corinthians 14:2 says when we pray in the spirit we do not speak to men, but to God, and although we don't understand exactly what we are praying, our spirit speaks mysteries.

After the third time he was released from the hospital, I received a call from him. The first thing he said to me was, "Do you want to know why I hate you?" I replied, "Yes, I have wondered that for a long time." His answer was, "Because you have so much peace."

Even though he hated me, I refused to hate him in return. It is possible to live at peace with others when they are hurtful toward you, but that didn't come automatically for me.

For the first few years of my

Christian life, I struggled with how to respond to my relatives because they weren't happy I had become a Christian. After diligently seeking the Lord about it, I realized that no matter how they viewed or treated me, I could remain at peace with them. But I must admit, it was work.

Some think the easy way out of a situation like that is to remove yourself from the person altogether. But if you don't face it now, there will only be another person that is more irritating to you somewhere down the road. Really, the easy way out of a situation is to conquer it once and for all and live the rest of your life with inner peace.

The *New Living Translation* says, "Turn away from evil and do good. Work hard at living in peace with others" (Psalms 34:14). Many times in order to live in peace with others, we must work hard at turning away from their evil and do good.

Will You Let Peace Rule?

When the enemy attacks you with strife, confusion or offense, if you will allow it, peace from your recreated spirit will rise up and settle the issue. But will you *let* peace rule? Or will you push peace aside and take matters into your own hands?

Notice Colossians 3:15 again,

Let the peace (soul harmony which comes) from Christ rule (act as an umpire continually) in your hearts [deciding and settling with finality all questions that arise in your minds, in that peaceful state] to which as [members of Christ's] one body you were also called [to live].

You choose whether you will let peace rule continually. That means your peace will be challenged. You must decide and settle with finality the fact that peace will rule in your mind regardless of circumstance. Make the decision to draw on the fruit of the spirit. Then when the challenge presents itself, yield to peace. You may only have a split second to decide, but that is all the time you need.

For instance, after a car pulls out in front of you, you have only a moment to either yield to peace or let the other driver have it with everything you've got. You decide. Why don't you make that decision now while you are not under attack? Then settle it with finality: "From this day forward, I will yield to peace."

Circumstances aren't always peaceful, but the peace of God can rule in any circumstance it is allowed to. Choose peace. Jesus was in the boat asleep when the disciples were upset because of the storm. Because peace was the umpire making the calls in every situation He faced, Jesus was able to speak peace to the storm. He never allowed the storm to get in His heart.

Psalm 63:8 says, "My soul followeth hard after thee" (*King James Version*). This speaks of a person pursuing something with all his or her heart! The picture here is of earnest desire and serious effort being given in order to stay in communion and peace with God. This person is following close behind God, unwilling to lose sight of Him.

Remember: Maintaining a peaceful heart is important not only to you, but also to a world that is in desperate need of peace. You must have peace in order for the world to draw upon it. You can be the one with a peaceful presence whom the family members call when there is trouble.

The same peace of God that reigned in Jesus can take you through any situation you face. Jesus never let the devil upset Him. On one occasion the Bible records an angry mob tried to push Him over a cliff. But right as they got to the edge, He turned and walked right through the midst of them. He remained at peace no matter what was happening around Him.

You Need Peace to Hear From God

You can learn to let peace rule inside when trouble breaks loose outwardly. That is what one of my favorite characters in the Bible did. Joseph was betrayed by everyone he trusted. If anyone had the right to shout "victim," he did all the more. But in spite of all the cruelty he endured, he never allowed it into his heart.

At the tender age of seventeen, he had a dream that

caused his brothers to hate him and plot to kill him. Although Joseph didn't understand the dream, he was quick to believe it. His brother, Judah saw no advantage in merely killing Joseph, so he decided to sell him into slavery. Potiphar, Joseph's new master could see the Lord was with Joseph—he had a peaceful spirit. He stood head and shoulders above the others. When Joseph was in charge of Potiphar's affairs, the Bible says things ran smoothly and flourished.

Mrs. Potiphar was bored with life and wanted to have an affair with Joseph, but he refused her. That didn't settle well with her, so she lied to her husband claiming

Joseph attacked her. That caused Joseph to be put in prison.

Such peace ruled in Joseph that he chose not to defend himself, fully assured God was in control. When asked by an inmate what he was doing time for, he answered, "I was stolen away from my family." He was cautious to guard his heart from words that would sway his heart toward bitterness and unforgiveness.

While in prison, the warden put all the affairs in Joseph's care. It says while Joseph was in charge of the prison affairs, everything prospered. Your heart attitude affects your prosperity. First Corinthians 13:3 says:

If I give all my possessions to feed the poor, and if I deliver my body to be burned, but do not have love, it profits me nothing.

The day came when Joseph stood before Pharaoh as the wisest man on earth. Unlike some claim, Joseph didn't go from prison to prime minister overnight—it took a lifetime of guarding his heart and a lifetime of refusing to harbor unforgiveness. The rewards were well worth the wait!

The dream God had given Joseph would never have manifested if he had chosen unforgiveness. Far too many people choose instant gratification rather than waiting for God's manifestation. Choosing to yield to the flesh may cause you to forfeit God's plan for your life. Had Joseph yielded to unforgiveness and strife, his heart might not have been quiet and peaceful enough to hear the interpretation of Pharaoh's dream. Your inner man must be quiet and peaceful to hear from God.

When Joseph's brothers traveled to Egypt to buy grain during the famine, it was his chance to repay them. He could have said, "I told you so," but he didn't. Instead he spoke these words from a peaceful spirit:

> I am your brother Joseph,
> whom you sold into
> Egypt. And now do not be
> grieved or angry with
> yourselves, because you
> sold me here; for God
> sent me before you to
> preserve life (Genesis
> 45:4-5).

Joseph had to work at not becoming bitter, just like you and I do. He wasn't endowed with some special ability that shielded him from hurt. He had feelings and emotions. He had to deny his flesh the privilege of becoming bitter. Every day he was separated from his father, his heart hurt. But he chose to dwell on the plan of God. The dream would never have manifested if he had chosen unforgiveness.

God Looks for the Quiet Heart

Second Chronicles 16:9 from *The Living Bible* says,

> For the eyes of the Lord search back and forth across the whole earth, looking for people whose hearts are perfect toward him, so that he can show his great power in helping them.

The word *perfect* in this verse

doesn't refer to performance. It means not only one whose heart is committed; but also, surprisingly, one whose heart is peaceful and quiet.

Choose to be that one whose heart is peaceful and quiet—the one for whom the eyes of the Lord search the whole earth. As you let peace guard your heart from every intruder and rule like an umpire in every situation, you will enjoy undisturbed fellowship with God. And you will give Him the opportunity to do what He desires most—show Himself strong on your behalf.

References

New American Standard Bible © The Lockman Foundation 1960, 1962, 1963, 1968, 1972, 1973, 1975, 1977, La Habra, California.

The Amplified Bible © The Lockman Foundation, La Habra, California, 1954, 1958.

The New Testament in Modern English (Phillips). Rev. Ed. © 1958, 1959, 1960, 1972 by J.B. Phillips. Published by Macmillan Publishing Co., New York, New York.

The Heart of Paul © 1976 by Ben Campbell Johnson. Published by A Great Love, Inc., Toccoa, Georgia.

Vikki Burke is the wife and ministry partner of Dennis Burke. Together they have affected thousands of people through a refreshing approach to God's Word.

Their ministry has taken them throughout the United States, as well as Australia, Asia, New Zealand, Canada and the United Kingdom.

Dennis and Vikki began in ministry as youth pastors in Southern California where they obtained tremendous insight into the work of the local church. In 1976, they moved to Fort Worth, Texas to work with Kenneth Copeland Ministries. Vikki worked with KCM for three years before entering full-time ministry with her husband.

Compelled by the love of God and the desire to see change in others, Vikki has delivered answers and insight to God's people. She has spoken at women's conferences, retreats, Bible studies, marriage seminars and the Fresh Fire™ television broadcast. Through the uncompromised Word of God, she has brought encouragement to many in the body of Christ.

People of Promise Are Impacting Lives!

Every day someone is being changed by the power of God's Word through Dennis Burke Ministries. Reports come into our office daily about how God's Word has brought healing, hope, restoration to a marriage or salvation to a loved one. The Word is producing fruit for the Kingdom of God!

Our Partners are a vital part of all the work we are doing. Every person who is changed through this ministry will have our Partners to thank. Partnership means that you join with us to impact people. Through your monthly giving of any amount, you can join with us today and multiply what God is doing to minister to people worldwide.

The *People of Promise* are people who have joined with this ministry through praying and monthly giving to help fulfill the Great Commission. When you join in Partnership, the anointing, favor and grace that rests on this ministry will rest upon you. When you have a need in your family, your business, your finances or whatever it might be, you can draw upon the anointing that operates in this ministry to help.

Also, as a Partner you will never be without prayer! Dennis and Vikki, as well as their staff pray for you. When you send your prayer requests we join our faith with yours for the anointing of God to remove every burden and destroy every yoke!

Even though our calling is to the world, our hearts are devoted to our Partners. That's why we designed a

Collector's Series exclusively for our Partners—*People of Promise*.

The Collector's Series gives our Partners the opportunity each month to receive an exclusive teaching tape in which we have added a personal prayer and message.

When you send your initial offering of $20.00 or more, you will receive a beautiful Collector's Series album and the first tape in the series. Each time you send your offering, you have the opportunity to receive the next month's tape in the series.

Join the *People of Promise* family by becoming a monthly Partner today. Fill out the coupon on the next page and enclose your first Partnership offering and we will link our faith with yours for God's best to be multiplied to you now!

Tear out the coupon and mail to: Dennis Burke Ministries, PO Box 150043, Arlington, TX 76015

I want to join Dennis and Vikki in fulfilling the Great Commission. Enclosed is my first offering to become a monthly Partner.

☐ $100   ☐ $ 50   ☐ $20   ☐ $____
                                      (Other)

☐ Please send my Collector's Series album and my first tape.

Name _____

Address _____

City_____

State _____ Zip_____

Phone (_____) _____

VISA or MasterCard Number:

_____

Expiration Date: _____

BOOKS BY
VIKKI BURKE

Aim Your Child Like An Arrow

Relief and Refreshing

AUDIO TAPES BY
VIKKI BURKE

*Pressing Through the Promise
into Possession*

*Burn with Passion—
Reach a Higher Level of Living*

VIDEO TAPES BY
VIKKI BURKE

God Likes Things Hot!

BOOKS BY DENNIS BURKE

*Dreams Really Do Come True—
It Can Happen to You!*

How's Your Love Life?

Develop A Winning Attitude

Breaking Financial Barriers

You Can Conquer Life's Conflicts

Grace: Power Beyond Your Ability

* How to Meditate God's Word

Knowing God Intimately

*A Guide to Successfully Attaining
Your God-given Goals*

The Law of the Wise

* Available in Spanish

AUDIO TAPES BY DENNIS BURKE

Creating an Atmosphere and Attitude for Increase

The Transfer of Wealth— Tearing Down Satan's Final Stronghold

The Tithe—Your Blessing Connection

Learning to Yield to the Holy Spirit

How to Cast Off Whatever Has Cast You Down

How to Bring Your Dreams to Life

Secrets to Developing Strength of Character

For a complete list of books, audio
and video cassettes by Dennis and
Vikki Burke or to receive their free
publication,
Words to the Wise write;

Dennis Burke Ministries
PO Box 150043
Arlington, TX 76015
(817) 277-9627

Feel free to include your prayer
requests when you write.

Visit our website at:
www.dennisburkeministries.org